BETRAYED FROM WITHIN

Surviving Bureaucratic Stress and Administrative Betrayal in Law Enforcement

Gina Gallivan, Ph.D., ABPP

Copyright © 2025 by Gina Gallivan, Ph.D., ABPP

All rights reserved. No part of this publication may be reproduced, stored in a retrieval system, or transmitted in any form or by any means — electronic, mechanical, photocopying, recording, or otherwise — without the prior written permission of the author, except in the case of brief quotations embodied in critical articles or reviews.

Published in the United States of America.

For information, contact:
Gina Gallivan
www.firstresponderpsych.com ISBN: 979-8-218-71299-0
Library of Congress Control Number: 2025912499

Printed in the United States of America
First Edition

Cover design by Robert Jarocki
Developmental Editing by Lia Ottaviano

This book is a work of nonfiction. Stories and examples are based on real events but have been modified to protect the privacy and confidentiality of those involved.

Dedication

To every first responder who carried the weight of injustice in silence—who was passed over, pushed out, or punished for doing the right thing.

This is for those who endured betrayal behind the badge and never got the acknowledgment, support, or closure they deserved.

May these pages be a form of validation—and a reminder that you weren't alone, even if it felt that way.

Disclaimer

All names used in first responder stories throughout this book are fictional or have been replaced with pseudonyms to protect the privacy and confidentiality of those involved. Any resemblance to actual persons, living or deceased, is purely coincidental.

Table of Contents

Introduction: The Real Trauma is Internal ix

Chapter 1: Death by a Thousand Cuts 1

Chapter 2: The Politics of Promotion 6

Chapter 3: When Discipline Depends on Who You Are 10

Chapter 4: The Checked-Out Captain and the Untouchable Toxic Leader 15

Chapter 5: The Promotion Personality Change 20

Chapter 6: The Weaponization of Policy 24

Chapter 7: Departments That Get It Right 30

Chapter 8: When Policy Hurts More Than Pediatric Death 34

Chapter 9: Bureaucracy and the Bottle 37

Chapter 10: Families Pay the Price, Too 40

Chapter 11: Healing from Administrative Betrayal 50

Chapter 12: Building a Culture That Doesn't Eat Its Own 55

Conclusion: You Can Heal Without Their Apology 65

Acknowledgments 73

References 78

Recommended Reading: You're Not Alone 81

Introduction: The Real Trauma Is Internal

"Nearly all men can stand adversity, but if you want to test a man's character, give him power."
— Abraham Lincoln

When officers talk about trauma, most people think of street-level threats: child death calls, fatal accidents, shootings. And while those events stay with you, they're not the ones that break most people. What wears you down—the part no one warns you about—is what happens inside the walls of your own department.

You start your career believing you've joined something bigger than yourself. A mission. A team. A family. And for a while, that holds true.

Then you begin to see the cracks:

- The guy who's popular and reckless gets a DUI and gets help. The one who keeps his head down and does the job gets the same DUI—and gets fired.

- The captain who's six months from retirement and refuses to engage because "he doesn't need the stress."

- The sergeant who was solid in the field, dependable, and loyal to his fellow officer, but the moment he was promoted, he started leading with fear, retaliation, and ego.

- The invisible weight of being passed over for promotion with no explanation—again.

This isn't burnout. It's betrayal. And it cuts deeper than most critical incidents because it doesn't end after a single call. **You live with it every shift, every month, every year.**

Some people numb out. Some get angry. Some walk away altogether. And some—far too many—start thinking they're the problem.

You're not. The system is.

This book goes beyond the visible dangers of police work to examine the internal pressures, betrayals, and disillusionments that quietly erode officers' well-being. It is a guide for recognizing the hidden organizational dynamics—misused authority, calculated silence, and ineffective leadership—that undermine morale and threaten the mission from within. It's about the officers who show up every day in environments that don't support them—and the damage that causes over time.

We're going to name the dynamics most people in this profession experience but don't talk about. We'll call out the double standards, the toxic promotions, the way accountability is applied inconsistently depending on who you are and who you know. And we'll talk about what it takes to survive that kind of environment without becoming cynical, numb, or self-destructive in the process. This book isn't just about what's wrong with the system. It's about how to keep yourself from being taken down by it.

Let's begin.

Chapter 1

Death by a Thousand Cuts

Before we dive in, a word about leadership.

If you're in a command position reading this, I want you to know that this book isn't about blame—it's about truth. Many chiefs and supervisors I've worked with are doing their absolute best under immense pressure. They're balancing politics, staffing shortages, lawsuits, and expectations from every direction. Some inherited broken systems. Some are running themselves into the ground trying to fix them. This book is not an attack. It's an acknowledgment of what your people may be experiencing quietly while still showing up for the mission. Leadership matters—and this book is written to help create environments where both the badge and the people wearing it can thrive.

I've sat across from good leaders who care deeply but feel trapped by broken systems, too. This book is for them as much as it is for the people they lead.

Now, let's talk about what's eroding the culture from the inside out.

Jeff used to love the job. The early mornings, the camaraderie, the feeling of purpose when he pinned on the badge. But after fifteen years, something began to shift.

It started small. A denied vacation request here. A sarcastic comment in briefing there. The kind of things you shrug off at first, tell yourself not to take personally. "It's just the job," Jeff reassured himself.

But then came the write-up for being five minutes late—on the same day his partner no-called, no-showed without consequence. Then his request to lateral into a specialty unit was denied without explanation, even though he'd been told he was next in line. The promotion list came out—and his name wasn't on it. The guy who golfs with the captain every Saturday? Top of the list.

At home, Jeff's wife asked what was wrong. He didn't have an answer. Because how do you explain that the job that used to give your life now drains it from you?

He wasn't burned out from the street. He could handle chaos, blood, and even grief. He'd built resilience for that. What he couldn't handle was the **institutional gaslighting**—being told to be honest and ethical, only to be punished for doing exactly that.

He stopped volunteering for overtime. Stopped mentoring the trainees. He still showed up, still did the job—but the spark was gone. And everyone could see it.

Jeff isn't broken. He's just exhausted by a system that talks about loyalty but doesn't practice it. And he's not alone.

Most officers don't break from one catastrophic event. It's not the worst call that causes them to throw in the towel. It's the relentless accumulation of everyday slights and injustices—the steady weight of feeling undervalued or ignored—that slowly wears them down. It's the chronic, internal stress—the thousand tiny betrayals that bleed them out slowly.

You expect trauma. You're trained for the chaos. What no one warns you about is the damage that comes from within your own walls. The kind that doesn't generate a use-of-force report or make the evening news. The kind that builds from inconsistent leadership, selective discipline, poor communication, or watching someone get away with something that would've ended your career.

You see it. You log it mentally. And over time, the job starts to feel different. Eventually, you catch yourself weighing every slight against the mounting toll—asking yourself if all the sacrifices, the sleepless nights, and the constant tightrope walk between duty and dignity are really worth the cost to your spirit.

It starts small:

- A promotion that goes to someone with less experience but the right friendships.
- A counseling memo you get for a minor issue while someone else gets a pass for something far worse.
- A policy that's enforced this week but ignored the next.
- A leader who smiles in front of the troops but retaliates quietly behind closed doors.

It doesn't feel like trauma. It feels like erosion. And there's no language for it. You can't file a report for betrayal. You can't clock out for "moral injury." So you push through. Tell yourself it's just politics. Try to shake it off. Until one day, you realize that you no longer trust the system.

You weren't naïve. You knew every department had its issues. But you believed that showing up with integrity, doing good work, and staying sharp would be enough.

You saw a colleague ask for support and get brushed off, their honesty met with distance instead of help. Leadership made big promises about wellness, but burnout quietly spread. People kept their struggles hidden, afraid that speaking up would make things worse. Little signs of neglect—ignored milestones, dismissed achievements—added up. Morale didn't just fall; it disappeared. You realized the real harm wasn't a single event, but the slow, steady loss of trust.

So, you adapted. You kept your head down. You disengaged—not because you were lazy, but because you were tired. Tired of the double standards. Tired of the silence. Tired of caring more than the people above you seem to.

And here's the truth most people don't want to say: **This kind of stress is often worse than a critical incident.**

Because it doesn't end. It isn't a one-time trauma. It's a constant, low-grade betrayal you carry with you—every day, every shift. You're not imagining it. And you're not alone.

If this sounds familiar, you're not "too sensitive." You're not weak. You're reacting to a culture that hasn't evolved fast enough to meet the emotional realities of the profession.

This kind of stress has a name: bureaucratic stress, or the unique strain that arises when navigating rigid hierarchies, unclear policies, or inconsistent expectations. And when paired with broken systems or poor leadership, it becomes something deeper: **administrative betrayal.** That term may hit hard. It's supposed to. Because until we name it, we can't fix it.

If you're a leader reading this, you might feel uncomfortable. That's okay. You may have inherited a broken structure. You may be doing your best under heavy political pressure with too little support. This isn't an attack—it's a call to awareness. A chance to look closely at what's happening under your watch, even if you didn't create it.

Your people are still showing up. But some are angry, numb, or going through the motions. Not because they don't care—but because they no longer feel seen, safe, or supported.

That can change. But not if we keep pretending it's not happening.

This book is here to tell the truth. To name the patterns. To help you protect yourself—without losing yourself. Because this isn't about blame. It's about honesty.

And honesty is where healing begins.

Chapter 2

The Politics of Promotion

There's no faster way to damage morale in a department than through promotions that feel inconsistent, unclear, or political. Most officers understand that not everyone gets promoted. They're not asking for favors. They just want to know that the system is fair.

When it's not—or even when it just feels like it's not—officers lose trust not just in the promotion process, but in leadership as a whole. This chapter dives into how the politics behind promotions can quietly erode trust and morale in a department. It explores why transparency and fairness matter—and what's at stake when those values are missing.

Behind the Badge: J-Rod's Story

J-Rod had been with the department for 16 years. He had a solid work history, no disciplinary issues, and strong performance evaluations. He trained new hires, took on tough calls, and showed up when it counted. He didn't seek attention, but his partners respected him.

He applied for sergeant. Twice. The first time, he didn't make it. He stayed professional and kept doing the work. But the second time, someone with a known pattern of performance issues was promoted instead. That officer had friends in the right places. He knew how to work a room.

J-Rod didn't get angry. He just pulled back. He stopped volunteering for extra duties. Stopped taking initiative. He still did the job well, but the extra effort—the heart—wasn't there anymore.

When someone asked if he'd apply again, he said, "Why? It's already decided before you walk into the room."

The department didn't just lose a candidate. They lost a quiet leader. No one in command ever asked him what had changed.

Officers pay attention to how promotions are handled. If they see decisions being made based on popularity, politics, or relationships instead of performance and leadership ability, it changes how they engage. Some of the most qualified people will stop trying.

They'll say things like:

- "It's not worth it."
- "You already know who they're going to pick."
- "If I have to play that game, I'm not interested."

These reactions echo throughout the department, shaping attitudes and engagement. When qualified people lose faith in the process, everyone feels the impact. Let's look at how this dynamic affected another officer's journey — Danielle's story.

Behind the Badge: Danielle's Story

Danielle was a strong officer with solid experience. She had completed specialized assignments, mentored younger officers, and consistently stepped up for her team. She studied hard and earned her promotion to sergeant.

But once the announcement went out, the whispers started:

- "She only got it because she's a female."
- "They had to check a box."

- "It's a diversity thing."

None of it was true. She'd outperformed others on the exam and the panel. She'd earned her spot. But instead of walking into a leadership role with support, she had to prove herself all over again, this time as a supervisor.

Danielle did everything right. But the stress of feeling like she had to constantly justify her position wore on her. Promotions come with pressure — but they shouldn't come with resentment from the people around you.

When people stop believing the process is fair, they stop believing in leadership. It's not just about who gets promoted. It's about the message it sends to everyone else.

This doesn't mean leadership is failing. It just means it's worth looking at how the process is being perceived. If people feel shut out, discouraged, or unsupported, they won't always say it — but they will act on it. They'll disengage. They'll withdraw. And in some cases, they'll leave.

Promotions shape the future of the organization. They show what behaviors are rewarded and what kind of leadership is valued. If the process is clear, consistent, and fair, people stay motivated. If it's political, unpredictable, or silent, people start opting out.

The fix isn't complicated. Be clear. Be transparent. Talk to people after the process is over — especially if they didn't make it. Let them know what to work on. Let them know they're seen.

Because when officers trust the process, they stay in it. And when they don't, you lose good people who might never say a word.

In the end, how promotions are handled tells everyone what truly matters within an organization. When the process is transparent and fair, people remain engaged and committed to the team's mission. But when fairness is questioned, trust begins to unravel—often quietly, but with real consequences. As we turn to the next chapter on discipline, we'll see how consistency and integrity in every decision, not just promotions, are vital to sustaining credibility in leadership.

Chapter 3

When Discipline Depends on Who You Are

Every department says they want accountability. Every officer wants it—until it lands on them or someone they like. Accountability sounds noble in policy manuals and speeches, a shared value held up as the foundation of trust. But in practice, it's uncomfortable. It can test loyalties and reshape relationships when real consequences arrive.

It's easy to agree on fairness in the abstract, but far harder when fairness challenges the status quo or calls out a favorite colleague. That tension is where the cracks begin—not from the absence of rules, but from the reluctance to apply them equally, regardless of rank or reputation.

What breaks trust isn't discipline itself—it's when discipline is **inconsistent**. When it depends on who you are, who you know, or how liked you are in the building. That's when people start shutting down.

The Double Standard

Let's talk about what officers actually see:

- One officer gets a DUI. He's well-liked, jokes around with command, and has been with the department forever. He gets help, support, and is quietly protected.

- Another officer gets a DUI. He's not as well-connected, more introverted, and has maybe had tension with a supervisor. He's swiftly suspended without pay and put under investigation. He gets no second chance, no support.

It's a mistake with two very different outcomes.

And people notice.

They might not say anything publicly. But privately, they're keeping score. They're noting who gets help and who gets shown the door. Over time, they stop trusting that integrity or performance matter more than politics.

Looking the Other Way

Sometimes it's not about who's punished—it's about who's *ignored*.

The supervisor who's counting the days to retirement and lets things slide because "it's not worth the fight." The lieutenant who avoids conflict and leaves the burden on the line-level sergeants. The problematic employee who's been moved around for years instead of being held accountable.

And what message does that send?

To the people doing the right thing, it feels like a gut punch. Why bother stepping up when no one else seems to be held to the same standard?

To the ones pushing the limits, it becomes a green light. They know nothing's going to happen, so they keep doing it.

That's how a culture starts to rot from the inside out. Not because bad people are everywhere, but because good people stop believing their effort matters.

Behind the Badge: Rosa's Story

Rosa was a squared-away officer. Detail-oriented, sharp in the field, and respected by her team. One day, Rosa responded to a chaotic domestic call. In the heat of the moment, she made a quick decision and guided a teenager outside before backup could arrive. Technically, this broke protocol, but her focus was on keeping everyone safe.

She owned it. Took responsibility. But she was still hit with a written reprimand.

Meanwhile, another officer had made a similar mistake months earlier—more serious, arguably—and nothing was done. That officer had a tight relationship with admin. The issue was brushed aside.

Rosa never complained. She stayed professional. But her tone changed. She trusted leadership a little less. She stopped volunteering for committees. She did her job—but the spark to do more started to fade.

That's what happens when discipline feels uneven. It doesn't just impact the person who's written up—it sends a message to everyone else.

The Hidden Injury: Moral Injury in Policing

What many officers experience in these situations isn't just frustration—it's a form of **moral injury**. Originally studied in military populations, moral injury refers to the internal conflict and emotional suffering that happens when someone witnesses or is forced to be part of something that violates their deeply held sense of right and wrong (Litz et al., 2009).

In law enforcement, moral injury can occur when officers feel betrayed by leadership, when justice isn't applied fairly, or when they're punished for acting in good faith. These moments shake their trust in the organization, in the mission, and sometimes in themselves.

Unchecked, moral injury can lead to depression, anger, withdrawal, and even suicidal ideation (Williamson, Murphy, & Greenberg, 2020). And unlike physical wounds, this type of psychological injury often goes unnoticed.

Fairness Isn't Optional

You don't have to be perfect. But you do have to be consistent. In moments when fairness is at stake, people can forgive honest mistakes. On the other hand, inconsistent standards begin to erode trust, leaving teams questioning their leaders and their own sense of purpose.

When discipline is fair—even when it stings—people can accept it. But when it feels arbitrary, political, or personal, it cuts deeper. It feels like betrayal. And that kind of betrayal doesn't go away just because someone keeps showing up to work.

It lingers. It shows up in disengagement, in low morale, in bitterness quietly passed from one academy class to the next. Over time, this invisible wound undermines the very culture that departments depend on for resilience and unity.

So what can be done to restore faith and foster real commitment? The answer lies in the example set by those who lead.

If You Lead, Lead the Standard

If you're in a position of authority, you set the tone. You don't have to swing the hammer hard—but you do have to swing it evenly.

Consistency in leadership lays the groundwork for trust, but turning principles into practice requires concrete actions. Here are some essential ways leaders can build and protect that trust:

- Be transparent when possible.
- Hold people accountable — regardless of status.
- And support those who've made mistakes but are willing to do the work to recover.

Most importantly: *don't just protect the people who are easy to like.*

Because your team is watching. And they're not just judging your decisions — they're deciding how much of themselves they're still willing to give.

In the end, the health of any organization relies not on the everyday choices and integrity of those at the helm. When leadership falters — through neglect or unchecked power — the cost is measured in lost trust, diminished spirit, and eroded culture. Recognizing these patterns is the first step toward change. In the next chapter, we'll explore real stories of those caught in the crosshairs of failed leadership — and what it takes to break the cycle and rebuild what was lost.

Chapter 4

The Checked-Out Captain and the Untouchable Toxic Leader

There are few things more demoralizing than leadership that just doesn't lead.

Sometimes it's passive. A captain counting the days to retirement who doesn't lift a finger—not because he's incapable, but because he doesn't want the stress. So problems pile up. Discipline gets dodged. Toxic personalities run unchecked while the rest of the team is left to deal with the fallout.

Other times, it's aggressive. A lieutenant who plays by their own rules, retaliates when questioned, and always finds cover from someone higher up. Complaints go nowhere. Whispers circulate. People say, "Watch your back." And everyone learns to stop speaking up.

Both styles destroy culture—but in different ways.

The *checked-out captain* creates chaos through neglect. The *untouchable toxic leader* creates it through control. And when good people get trapped under either, it's a slow erosion of morale, trust, and identity.

You start to second-guess yourself. You watch the wrong people get promoted, the right people leave, and the worst behavior get excused. You start to realize that it's not competence that gets rewarded—**it's politics**.

When leadership drifts into indifference or unchecked authority, the ripple effects touch everyone. In this chapter, we'll see how these dynamics play out in real-world environments—where the line between healthy teamwork and dysfunction is often determined by the tone set at the top. Let's begin with a story that reveals just how personal and costly the consequences can become when those in power lose sight of what true leadership means.

A Real Story: The Cost of Crossing the Wrong Person

Sergeant Andrews wasn't confrontational by nature. He was respected, even-keeled, and known for keeping the peace. But one day, he pushed back on a directive from his lieutenant—respectfully, but in front of others.

The room went still. A few officers nodded quietly. Someone even smirked. The lieutenant didn't like being questioned, but he *hated* being questioned publicly. That moment wounded his pride—and like many leaders driven more by ego than ethics, he didn't forget it. He didn't move on. Instead, he waited.

And then, **he made it personal.** Sergeant Andrews' schedule was the first thing to change. His long-standing request to have Saturday mornings off to coach his son's soccer games—something that had never been a problem—was suddenly denied. Every single Saturday, he was assigned. No flexibility. No discussion.

Next came the sabotage. When the sergeant tried to lateral to another department to escape the tension, the lieutenant quietly made sure it didn't happen. Backchannel calls. Off-the-record comments. Enough shade to stop the process cold. No explanation. Just radio silence from the receiving agency.

Sergeant Andrews wasn't just denied a fresh start. **Rather, he was punished for wanting one.**

This wasn't about leadership. This was about control.

And in environments where power becomes an end in itself, no one is truly safe—not even those who play by the rules. When authority is used to settle scores, the organization trades its integrity for insecurity. The cost is measured not just in lost talent, but in the erosion of trust, teamwork, and the sense of fairness that make a department a place people want to be part of.

When Retaliation Targets Family, It Crosses a Line

Retaliation is always damaging—but when it targets someone's children, it crosses an ethical line that borders on the sociopathic.

We've seen it happen: A sergeant pushes back on a policy, and suddenly his shift is changed, preventing him from coaching his child's soccer team—like in the case of Sergeant Andrews.
Or a respected officer applies for a transfer, and instead of confronting him directly, the lieutenant targets his daughter—who works as a dispatcher in the same department—by manipulating her shifts and assignments to send a clear message.

Silent sabotage. Schedule manipulation. Punishment through proximity.

These are not minor acts. They are psychological weapons, designed to cause pain where it's most personal. And they reveal a level of emotional detachment—and cruelty—that should give any leader pause.

If you are using someone's family to make a point, to "put them in their place," or to punish them for challenging your authority, **you need to look in the mirror.** That's not discipline. That's abuse of power. And it's not leadership. It's a red flag for organizational dysfunction that damages morale, trust, and retention.

Departments that tolerate this behavior, even silently, risk losing not just good officers — but their humanity.

And here's what we know: When individuals in power display **narcissistic traits** — such as hypersensitivity to criticism, a need for admiration, and a lack of empathy — they often respond to perceived slights with retaliation rather than reflection (Rosenthal & Pittinsky, 2006). In these environments, rank becomes armor — and anyone who threatens the illusion gets targeted.

The Deeper Damage

This kind of leadership breakdown does more than frustrate. It creates moral injury. Officers are trained to follow a chain of command, to respect structure, to trust that their agency will have their back. When that trust is broken — not by one incident, but by years of inaction or abuse — it chips away at your purpose.

You don't feel proud anymore. You feel stuck. Like you're in a place that values power over people — and where calling something out puts a bigger target on your back than doing the wrong thing in the first place.

In real life, administrative betrayal can take many different forms. It might look like:

- Watching a colleague be tormented by a toxic supervisor while nobody steps in.
- Seeing leadership promote someone with a known history of retaliation.
- Being ignored after doing everything "right."

You're not going crazy or overreacting. It's not just a bad day. It's **death by a thousand cuts**—and many of those cuts come from leadership that failed to show up.

Before You Say "That's Not Me"

If you're reading this as a supervisor, commander, or aspiring leader—and you're thinking, *"I'm nothing like that lieutenant"*—pause. Ask yourself:

- Have people close to you ever told you that you lack empathy?
- That you overreact to being challenged?
- That you hold grudges or get stuck in power struggles?
- That your ego shows up more than your humility?

Sometimes the signs aren't loud. Sometimes they're in the subtle feedback you dismiss—because it doesn't fit how you see yourself. But here's the truth: **The higher you climb, the harder it is to hear the truth.** And the more power you hold, the more damage you can do without even realizing it.

So if you've ever been told those things—**listen.** Not with defensiveness. With courage. Because leaders who are willing to confront their own blind spots are the ones who build trust instead of fear.

Chapter 5

The Promotion Personality Change

There's nothing wrong with ambition. Some of the best leaders in law enforcement started with a deep desire to make things better—to lead by example, to take care of their people. They promoted for the right reasons.

But something happens on the climb. They get pulled into the politics. They start watching their backs. They stop pushing back and start playing the game. And eventually, they become what they once swore they wouldn't.

It's not uncommon to hear an officer say, "*He used to be one of us. I don't even recognize him anymore.*" One day, you're working side by side, chasing the same calls, venting about the same nonsense. The next day, they get promoted—and suddenly, the air shifts. The jokes stop. The radio gets quieter. You walk into the same room, but now you're treated like you don't belong.

The uniform didn't change them. The *rank* did.

The Shift No One Talks About

The personality change after promotion is one of the most disorienting parts of department culture. You thought you knew someone. But suddenly:

- They stop returning your texts.
- They start echoing the admin's talking points.
- They enforce policies they used to roll their eyes at.

And it's not just disappointing. **It's betrayal.** Because when someone forgets where they came from, everyone who came with them feels abandoned. You start to wonder if those late-night calls and shared frustrations meant anything at all. The camaraderie that once held you together unravels, replaced by a sense of being left behind by someone you thought would always have your back.

What Power Reveals

Some pass the test of leadership. They stay grounded. They remember what it's like to write reports at 2 a.m., do CPR on a baby, and spend Thanksgiving night in the report writing room. They lead with empathy and stay close to the work.

But for others, promotion becomes the mask that hides their insecurity—or worse, amplifies their ego. According to Keltner (2016), power tends to reduce empathy, increase impulsivity, and inflate people's sense of their own competence. Narcissistic traits—like entitlement, hypersensitivity to criticism, and a need to dominate—can become magnified once someone has authority without accountability.

And in departments where political alliances matter more than character, those traits don't just go unchecked. **They get rewarded.**

Behind Closed Doors

We've all witnessed it or heard the whispers—real stories from the field that don't show up in any official report:

- A newly promoted sergeant who talks down to the people he used to drink coffee with.
- A lieutenant who uses policy like a baseball bat to punish, not protect.
- A captain who's so afraid of rocking the boat, he does nothing—no matter how toxic the crew gets.

The worst part? Most of them weren't always like this. Sometimes, people start out grounded and genuine, but as they rise, their focus shifts to protecting their new status instead of supporting their team. When power turns into a shield, real leadership is lost.

This is a reminder for everyone—leaders and organizations alike—to stay alert to these pitfalls and remember why leadership matters in the first place. By facing these issues honestly, we set the stage for real change. Now, let's look at what happens when promotions reward politics over true leadership—and how that affects everyone.

Promotions Without Leadership and the Courage to Stay Humble

Here's the hard truth: the promotion system doesn't always select for the right traits. It rewards those who play the game well—those who know how to memorize policy, say the right thing in interviews, and avoid stepping on the wrong toes. And when people promote to escape the job—not lead it—it shows.

Because leadership requires more than book smarts. It requires emotional intelligence. It requires humility. It requires the self-awareness to admit when you're wrong—and the courage to course-correct.

In broken systems, the badge on your collar can start to matter more than the badge on your chest. And when that happens, **trust dies quietly.**

If you're in a leadership position and you're reading this, ask yourself:

- Do people still feel safe being honest with me?
- Do I take criticism as a threat—or a mirror?

- Do I make time for the people doing the hard work, or only the ones who flatter me?

Do people feel seen around you? Or just… evaluated? Think carefully about your answer and try to respond honestly. It's easy to say, "*I haven't changed.*" But the people around you might say otherwise.

If someone close to you—your spouse, your best friend, your team—has ever hinted that you're harder to talk to now, more reactive, less grounded, or wrapped up in status, listen. Not with shame. With honesty. Because the leaders who are willing to check their ego are also those who still have the respect of the people when the bars come off.

Getting promoted isn't the problem. **Forgetting who you were before the promotion is.**

The best leaders don't let power dilute their integrity. They don't forget the struggle just because they've reached the other side. They make sure the door stays open for the ones coming up behind them.

That's leadership. And no title on earth can fake it.

This chapter has demonstrated how the misuse of authority and selective enforcement of policies compromise trust, undermine morale, and foster a culture of fear and disillusionment. But it has also highlighted the path forward: remembering our roots, valuing transparency, and leading with humility.

As we move into the next chapter, we'll explore how these dynamics of power and policy not only affect individuals but shape the very culture of our organizations—and what it takes to restore faith in the systems designed to support us all.

Chapter 6

The Weaponization of Policy

There's a moment when you realize the rules aren't really about fairness—they're about control.

You see it when an officer with political protection gets a quiet pass, while someone else gets hammered for the same mistake. You feel it when policies designed to support wellness or safety are manipulated to discredit or sideline people who speak up. What should be a system of structure and support starts feeling like a setup.

When the real purpose of the rules becomes clear, trust erodes fast. Officers start to wonder if policies are really about fairness, or just tools for those in charge to protect themselves and shut down dissent. This chapter digs into how policy can be used as a weapon—from playing favorites to punishing anyone who doesn't fit in. We'll look at real examples of unequal discipline and the lasting impact on a department's culture. By the end, you'll see how these problems take hold and what it takes to start fixing them.

Now, let's look at one of the clearest signs of this problem: selective discipline, where double standards quietly destroy trust.

Selective Discipline: The Double Standard

You're late once, after years of solid performance, and it's immediately documented. Meanwhile, others show up late regularly with no consequence. Why? Because they're connected. Because they know how to play the game.

Or consider the officer who volunteers for extra shifts, covers holidays, and rarely calls in sick. One day, they respectfully question a new scheduling policy during roll call. Within a week, they're reassigned to a less desirable post—one everyone knows is a dumping ground for those who've fallen out of favor.

Meanwhile, another officer, who's open about their close friendship with a supervisor, regularly swaps shifts at the last minute and takes unscheduled days off. There's never a word of reprimand, just quiet accommodations.

This isn't accountability. This is favoritism enforced through selective discipline. And officers see it. They talk about it. And when it becomes the norm, trust dies quietly.

Departments encourage officers to seek help when struggling. The message is clear: "Use your resources. Take care of your mental health."

But what happens after an officer does? He's pulled from his assignment. Suddenly deemed a liability. Maybe even subjected to a fitness-for-duty evaluation that seems more punitive than supportive.

Peers whisper. Supervisors grow distant. The very system that told him to speak up now treats him like he's broken. It creates a chilling effect and sends a dangerous message: **If you show vulnerability, you'll be punished for it.**

Paper Trails and Petty Power Plays

Policy can be used to create structure and safety or to exact quiet retaliation. In the wrong hands, rules intended to uphold fairness can become instruments of control, wielded to settle scores or silence dissent. The line between legitimate oversight and punitive maneuvering grows blurry, leaving officers uncertain about whether their actions will be met with support or reprisal.

A sergeant questions a leadership decision during a briefing. Two days later, he's written up for a minor uniform infraction. An officer makes a legitimate complaint through the proper channels. Her transfer paperwork stalls with no explanation. A commander doesn't like the way someone challenged his authority. That officer gets pulled from specialty assignments and passed over for training opportunities.

These aren't coincidences. They're power plays. And because they're often wrapped in policy, they're harder to prove, harder to fight, and easier to deny.

Real Story: When a Performance Plan Isn't About Performance

There was an officer — let's call him Officer Marcos — who had served his community for decades. He wasn't flashy or political — just a steady presence in the field. But as the department came under new leadership with a vision to modernize and increase productivity, he started to feel the shift.

Officer Marcos had about 18 months left until retirement. By his own admission, he was no longer a high-output producer. He carried the weight of unresolved trauma — likely PTSD — and knew he wasn't the same officer he used to be. But he still showed up. Still served. Still tried.

Then the paperwork started.

He received comments on his evaluations hinting at "declining motivation" and "lack of engagement." He was placed on a Performance Improvement Plan. And after an incident where he spent extended time assisting a man who appeared impaired and was lying in the park, he returned to the station complaining of shortness of breath and chest tightness.

He asked to see a doctor, concerned about his health. It turned out he had undiagnosed allergies — something that had quietly impacted him for years. His doctor prescribed treatment that finally gave him relief. He left the appointment feeling better than he had in a long time.

But when he returned to work, no one asked how the appointment went. No one checked in. They didn't want an update—they wanted him out. He was told to turn in his badge and gun. He was being sent for a fitness-for-duty evaluation.

What had been a physical health issue—one that was improving—was interpreted as a psychological liability. But the fallout didn't end there.

The emotional toll of being quietly pushed out—after years of service—was too much. His stress spilled into his home. He became increasingly withdrawn and bitter. His wife, who had stood by him through so much, finally left—unable to tolerate the emotional weight he carried from a department that had once been his second family.

He wasn't just grieving a job. He was grieving the way it ended. And while we won't go into details, the way this story ended was tragic. It didn't have to be.

Real Story: The Transfer That Never Happened

There was a sergeant—we'll call him Raul—who had a strong reputation and a clean service record. He was known for mentoring younger officers, spending time with his young children, and staying out of department politics.

But one day, he pushed back—respectfully but firmly—against a lieutenant's decision in a leadership meeting. The room got quiet. The lieutenant didn't say much. But others smirked. And Raul knew it didn't sit well.

Weeks later, he was reassigned to a less desirable shift—weekend nights—causing him to miss out on valuable time with his family. It wasn't a coincidence. It was personal.

Then came the transfer request. He'd applied for an open position in a specialized unit. On paper, he was the top candidate. But nothing happened. No follow-up. No denial. Just silence.

Informally, he heard that the lieutenant had "expressed concerns." That was all it took. His career momentum stalled. His reputation shifted. All because he spoke up once.

And because policy was flexible enough to cover personal retaliation, no one had to own it.

Clinical Sidebar: Betrayal and Moral Injury

What officers experience in these moments isn't just frustration—it's a psychological injury.

According to Litz et al. (2009), **moral injury** occurs when an individual feels betrayed by a trusted authority. In law enforcement, this often surfaces when officers are punished for doing the right thing, or when policies are manipulated to harm rather than help.

Moral injury isn't always loud. It's often experienced as a slow erosion of belief in the mission. Officers stop trusting leadership, stop speaking up, and disconnect emotionally from the work. This kind of betrayal doesn't just lead to burnout—it can lead to depression, substance use, and a deep sense of isolation (Papazoglou & Andersen, 2014).

Restoring Integrity: Leadership's Role in Healing

For some officers, it's not one big trauma that breaks them. It's the way they're treated when they're at their most vulnerable— by the very institution they gave their life to.

Policy isn't the problem. But when it's used as a weapon— selectively enforced, politically manipulated, or deployed in retaliation—it becomes a tool of organizational harm.

And the result? Officers no longer feel safe inside their own department. Leadership must understand: fair enforcement of policy isn't just about risk management. It's about culture. When the culture loses integrity, everything downstream — performance, morale, trust — begins to break down.

Policies should protect the mission, not just the administration. And if we're serious about retention, wellness, and culture change, we have to stop hiding behind the rulebook and start leading with courage.

The lesson is clear: authentic leadership is not about enforcing rules for their own sake, but about building trust, restoring dignity, and creating a culture where everyone feels valued. Departments that embrace this mindset spark genuine, lasting change that ripples outwards into every corner of their organization.

Let's now turn our attention to departments that are charting a new course — where leadership is redefining the culture from within, building trust, fostering genuine connection, and proving that transformation is possible when people, not just policies, come first.

Chapter 7

Departments That Get It Right

Not every department is broken. And not every leader turns a blind eye.

There are agencies out there — quietly, courageously — choosing to lead differently. They're not just checking boxes with wellness programs or hanging a motivational poster in the hallway. They're actually doing the work.

And it shows.

Santa Ana PD: Healing From the Inside Out

Santa Ana PD had been through a lot. Like many departments, the stress wasn't just coming from the street — it was coming from within. There was deep mistrust, fractured communication, and unspoken resentment between the upper command staff. The kind of internal tension that bleeds into morale, performance, and overall culture.

Then a new chief stepped in. And instead of ignoring the tension or managing it from a distance, he did something rare — he leaned in.

One of his commanders had the courage to step up and organize something unheard of: a three-day leadership retreat, designed not to push policy or teach tactics, but to repair what was broken — **the relationships** between the people leading the department.

They didn't start with rank. They started with a **story**

Each command staff member shared their personal history — where they came from, what shaped them, and what they carried. One by one, they began to see each other as people again—not just positions or titles. Walls came down. Common ground emerged. There were tears, silence, and eventually, laughter.

But the turning point was what came next.

The chief, without ego or defensiveness, stood before his team and **took ownership.** Not for a crime or scandal, but for the moments he could've shown up better. For the leadership misses, the silences, the decisions that may have hurt people, even if unintentional. He modeled what accountability looks like—not from a place of fear, but from humility.

Then each person followed. One by one, they owned their part. They named the harm, admitted their blind spots, and gave each other space to speak honestly. And then—something remarkable happened.

They healed.

By the end of the retreat, they weren't just coworkers again. They were a team. There were hugs. Apologies. Conversations that had needed to happen for years. And not in a forced, "team-building" kind of way—but a human one.

What Made It Work?

Their transformation wasn't accidental—it was the result of deliberate choices and practices that fostered trust and healing. Here are the core elements that made the retreat a catalyst for real change:

- **Intentional Leadership**: A chief who didn't have to be the smartest or strongest in the room—but chose to be *real*.

- **Courageous Facilitation**: A commander who dared to disrupt business as usual and create space for truth-telling.

- **Spiritual Connection**: The retreat included a chaplain, fireside chats, and time for reflection. This wasn't just about morale—it was about healing.

- **Shared Vulnerability**: They didn't just talk trust. They *built it*—on a hike, through eye contact, by listening to each other's pain.

- **Applied Skills**: Alongside bonding, they learned real communication skills—how to listen, how to apologize, how to rebuild what had been lost.

This wasn't a wellness retreat. It was leadership rehab—and it worked. In the end, what they gained was more than restored morale—it was a renewed sense of purpose, belonging, and hope for the future.

Why It Works: The Research Behind the Reform

Before diving deeper, it's important to understand the foundational practices that enabled such a profound transformation. The following core elements served as pillars for the retreat's success:

- **Psychological Safety**, the #1 predictor of high-performing teams, comes from shared vulnerability and mutual respect (Edmondson, 1999). Santa Ana PD created that space—and it changed everything.

- **Trust isn't built through policy—it's built through behavior.** According to Kouzes and Posner (2017), trust in leadership grows when leaders are willing to admit mistakes and model accountability.

- **Narrative psychology** shows that sharing life stories enhances empathy, reduces conflict, and increases perceived connection—especially in high-stakes professions (McAdams, 2001).

- And finally, **trauma recovery**—both individual and organizational—requires space for truth, validation, and rebuilding meaning (Herman, 1992). Santa Ana's process mirrored this exactly.

Departments don't fall apart because of one bad incident. They corrode slowly—through silence, ego, avoidance, and fear. But healing doesn't have to take decades. It just takes someone willing to go first.

Santa Ana PD's story reminds us: culture isn't fixed. It's forged. And when leaders lead with courage, departments don't just survive—they transform. Some departments are also making progress in smaller but meaningful ways, like hosting wellness days for overworked officers, offering optional debriefs, embedding culturally competent clinicians, or opening the door to honest conversations about stress and trauma.

These efforts matter. They plant seeds. But few examples go as deep—or as transformational—as what Santa Ana PD dared to do. They didn't just run a program. They led with humility. And they changed the culture—not by force, but by facing the pain together.

That's what it looks like when a department gets it right.

Chapter 8
When Policy Hurts More Than Pediatric Death

Officers have been trained to handle the unimaginable. They stand at the side of grieving parents during pediatric deaths. They deliver death notifications. They fight to save children. These calls leave scars.

But here's the truth: **many officers say what happens *inside* their departments hurts more.**

In our original dataset of sworn law enforcement officers, we asked a brutal question: "If you've experienced both a pediatric death call and administrative betrayal or bureaucratic stress, which impacted your psychological health more?"

Officers didn't hesitate to answer—and their answers confirmed what we'd suspected all along.

The Data That Changes the Narrative

We calculated two indexes from officer responses:

- A **BSAB Index** (Bureaucratic Stress and Administrative Betrayal), which included how often admin issues impacted morale, trust in leadership, perceived support, and whether they considered quitting.

- A **PDC Index** (Pediatric Death Call Trauma), which measured emotional impact, trauma symptoms, and support following those incidents.

The average scores were nearly identical:

- **BSAB Index Mean:** 11.97

- **PDC Index Mean:** 12.61

This means that, on average, **officers rated the emotional impact of internal betrayal and red tape nearly as high as the trauma of witnessing the death of a child.**

Let that land for a moment.

This is a profession where you *expect* trauma. But you don't expect it from your own department. When the call comes from inside the house, the injury cuts deeper — and it's harder to heal. Recognizing this is the first step toward real solutions.

The Hidden Wound: Moral Injury from Within

Administrative betrayal often includes:

- **Unequal discipline:** For example, two officers make the same mistake, but only one faces suspension while the other receives a warning.

- **Lack of backing during controversial calls:** After a split-second decision on the street, leadership issues a public statement distancing themselves from the officer without reviewing all the facts.

- **Promotion gamesmanship:** Despite years of service and exemplary evaluations, an officer is passed over for promotion in favor of someone with closer ties to command.

- **Being thrown under the bus by command staff:** When a community complaint arises, supervisors quickly blame the officer involved to appease the public, rather than conducting a fair internal review.

These aren't just grievances. They're wounds to an officer's moral core—the belief that their department will have their back.

As one officer put it, "I knew the job would be dangerous. I didn't know the enemy would be upstairs."

Implications for Wellness

This data should help broaden our understanding of what trauma looks like in policing. Beyond the visible dangers of the street, officers often face another, quieter form of harm—one inflicted from within their own institutions.

Departments that only fund debriefings after child deaths but ignore internal dysfunction are missing the real source of burnout. When leadership fails to address problems within their own walls, it sends a message that officer wellness is not a priority. Real change starts with honest conversations about what's happening inside, not just what's faced outside.

Officers aren't quitting because the job is hard. They're quitting because the **support structure is broken.** When trust in leadership crumbles, even the strongest sense of duty can start to crack. Without real support from inside, resilience becomes nearly impossible to sustain.

We must include **administrative betrayal** in the trauma-informed care conversation. And as this study shows, sometimes the hardest part of the job isn't death. It's what happens after you survive it—and no one upstairs shows up.

Note: The data presented in this chapter were collected and analyzed by the author as part of a larger research initiative through the Police Officer Wellness Initiatives Committee of the International Association of Chiefs of Police (IACP). A formal publication is in progress in collaboration with fellow committee members.

Chapter 9

Bureaucracy and the Bottle

They'll tell you it's about the trauma. The scenes. The screams. The blood. The death. And yes, that's part of it. But it's not the whole story. The quiet truth—the one we rarely talk about in command briefings or peer support sessions—is this: **Many officers aren't drinking to numb the horrors of the street.** They're drinking to numb the betrayal inside the building.

The weaponized policy. The silent retaliation. The years of being overlooked, micromanaged, passed over, and disrespected by leaders who know how to quote values—but not how to live them.

They're not just drinking to forget the dead kids or the bloody scenes. They're drinking to forget how it feels to be discarded. Disrespected. To be micromanaged by someone who's never done the job. To give everything to a department that gives nothing back.

And because this kind of betrayal can't be talked about—not without fear of being labeled, isolated, or disciplined—officers do what they've been conditioned to do: **they internalize it**. They bottle it up. And then—**they drink their poison.**

They don't realize that what they're swallowing isn't just alcohol—it's all the bitterness, the resentment, the moral injury they were never allowed to process. The poison isn't the whiskey. The poison is everything they're forced to keep inside.

Whiskey and Country Music: Numbing the Narrative

It's 4 a.m. and the shift is done. The trainee's gone home. The reports are filed. And one seasoned officer sits in his kitchen, nursing a bottle of whiskey while country music plays low in the background.

It sounds cliché—until you realize how common it is. The music tells the truth they can't speak, can't communicate to even those closest to them. Songs about betrayal, loss, identity, and escape. Stories of good men pushed too far. Of silent pain. Of the kind of pride that makes asking for help impossible.

Alcohol translates the pain. It communicates, "I'm not okay," without requiring its user to admit it out loud. It creates a moment of stillness where one can feel *something* without the risk of being judged. For many, it's the only time their nervous system slows down. For some, it's the only place they feel in control. And for others—it's the beginning of the end.

The Bureaucratic Loop

When the system punishes its best, protects the worst, and gaslights the ones in the middle, officers don't just burn out—they **check out**. They lose faith in leadership. In justice. In the mission. And that loss doesn't just live in their minds. It seeps into their bodies. Their marriages. Their habits.

According to the research, organizational stressors are more predictive of officer distress than operational ones (Violanti et al., 2017). Meaning: what happens **inside the department** often causes more emotional damage than what happens on the street.

Even officers with no prior substance issues may start drinking more frequently in response to perceived organizational injustice (Shane, 2010). When betrayal becomes routine, alcohol becomes a sedative, a shield, a middle finger to a system that no longer sees them.

Clinical Sidebar: When Moral Injury Fuels Misuse

Research supports that alcohol misuse among first responders is often rooted not just in trauma exposure but in moral injury — the betrayal of what they believe to be right by those in power (Papazoglou & Andersen, 2014; Litz et al., 2009).

When an officer is disciplined for trying to do the right thing, denied backup by a supervisor with a grudge, or forced into a fitness-for-duty evaluation as retaliation, they don't just feel hurt. They feel violated. And when that sense of violation is left unspoken, officers often retreat into themselves. What follows isn't just a bad mood or a tough day — it's a gradual slide into increased alcohol use, sleep disruption, emotional numbing, and, in some cases, suicidality (Violanti, 2020). These aren't signs of weakness; they're signals that something inside the system is broken, and real support is needed to help officers heal.

The Hidden Toll of Organizational Betrayal

If we keep treating officer wellness as a resilience issue instead of a leadership issue, we'll keep losing good people. The bottle isn't the problem. It's the symptom. And until we address the organizational betrayal, toxic command culture, and silence around moral injury, we're not solving the real problem. You can't write a policy that fixes betrayal.

But you can build a culture where officers don't have to drink just to survive their shift.

This chapter has delved into the hidden costs of organizational betrayal, showing how wounds inflicted by leadership and institutional culture can drive officers toward isolation, substance use, and worse. As we turn to Chapter 9, the scope widens: we follow these wounds home, examining how the same forces that debilitate officers from within also fracture families and quietly reshape life beyond the badge.

Chapter 10

Families Pay the Price, Too

Officer Paulson walks in the door at 7:45 a.m., still in uniform. Not because he forgot to change, but because his mind is still on the job. Still in that office. Still stuck in the sting of being written up again for something petty. Still replaying how his supervisor, who's never once walked a mile in his boots, denied his time-off request with a smirk.

His wife is feeding the baby, scrolling Instagram with one hand, bottle in the other. She sees him — but not really. He's there, but the light's gone. And she knows it.

Officer Paulson's distance isn't about a hard call or a traumatic scene. It's about his slow erosion of self-worth from working under leadership that punishes integrity and rewards obedience. It's about the type of betrayal that doesn't make the news, but makes it impossible to come home whole.

Officer Paulson doesn't talk about the snide remarks in briefing. Or the shift change he got after reporting a safety concern. Or how the promotion went to someone who plays the game, not someone who earned it.

Instead, he goes quiet. Not because he's coping with trauma, but because he knows talking won't change anything — and might make it worse.

So he nods when his wife asks him a question, not really listening to what she's said. He pretends that he's okay and internalizes his pain.

Home becomes just another performance. One more place he has to "keep it together." His family doesn't get his worst — they get his nothing. His wife used to ask questions. Now she doesn't. The kids used to run to the door when he came home. Now they pause, reading his face like it's a weather report. The man who once coached their soccer games now scrolls his phone or zones out in front of the TV, still in uniform, still somewhere else.

He's not snapping because of a call. He's short-tempered because he's trapped in a system that punishes truth-tellers and rewards those who play the game.

But even in the shadow of betrayal, a little honesty still goes a long way. Saying, "It's been a rough week. The politics at work are getting to me," is better than silence. Because otherwise, his wife just thinks: "Why is he so angry all the time?"

That one sentence can shift her from feeling rejected to feeling compassion. It doesn't fix the system—but it protects the relationship.

The Fallout of Retaliation

When the department retaliates—through gossip, discipline, or transfer games—it doesn't just demoralize the employee. It sends shockwaves into the home.

The partner starts resenting the job. The kids stop asking when Dad will be home. The marriage becomes about logistics, not love. Everyone walks on eggshells because they're all absorbing the stress he can't speak aloud.

Children learn what power looks like by watching how their parents are treated. They see the toll it takes when Dad is overlooked, disrespected, or silenced. They internalize it.

They see how you react to unfairness. To power used poorly. To systems that break good people. They watch how you treat others, how you carry your pain, and how you show up when you're experiencing it—whether you retreat from it or acknowledge and work through it.

You are teaching your children what to expect from a future partner. They will seek what's familiar. Make what you model something they can count on.

And if they don't see their parent fighting for their self-worth — or naming that something's wrong — they might grow up thinking this is just what adulthood looks like: silent suffering.

So even if you're emotionally wrecked — show up. Be early. Be consistent. Be steady. Not perfect. Just accountable.

What Actually Helps

Dr. Kevin Gilmartin recommends a 20-minute transition period between shift and home life. It's sound advice. But when betrayal follows you off-duty, even 20 minutes won't cut it unless the pain is named.

When facing the weight of departmental politics, it's easy to feel powerless or isolated. Yet, even in the midst of emotional exhaustion, there are concrete ways to reclaim your agency and support your loved ones. The following actions are practical steps you can take to begin healing, restore trust, and model resilience for your children and partner:

- Say, "I had a hard day. Not from the street — from the politics."
- Let your partner in without dumping the whole file.
- Don't let resentment take root in silence.
- Get support — not just for trauma, but for betrayal. Moral injury needs its own healing path.

Recognizing and naming the impact of betrayal is the first step toward real recovery. By showing up honestly for ourselves and our families, even when it's uncomfortable, we interrupt cycles of silent suffering and model resilience for those who look up to us. As we move forward, let's look at how these struggles play out in specific moments, and what happens when betrayal strikes close to home.

For Those Navigating Divorce and Custody

For first responders who are co-parenting after divorce, the trauma doesn't end when the marriage does—but how you show up for your kids still matters. In fact, it may matter more than ever.

The absolute worst thing that can happen to a child is abandonment. And it doesn't have to be dramatic or intentional. It can be missing a visit. Being late—again. Cancelling at the last minute. Making a child feel like they're not a priority.

In fact, research shows that emotional neglect and psychological maltreatment can be just as harmful—or even more harmful—than physical abuse. Studies have found that emotional abuse and abandonment are strongly associated with depression, anxiety, substance use, and long-term relational difficulties, sometimes with greater negative impact than physical or sexual abuse (Spinazzola et al., 2014; Teicher & Samson, 2016).

The American Academy of Pediatrics has also emphasized that emotional maltreatment—including abandonment—is linked to significant disruptions in brain development and can contribute to a lifetime of emotional instability and vulnerability.

Quality time with your children doesn't require extravagant plans. What they need most is consistency, predictability, and emotional presence. That starts with the basics:

- Stick to the same days and times every week. Kids thrive on routine. Avoid rescheduling unless it's truly unavoidable.

- Never miss a scheduled visit. Follow through. No matter what.

- Be on time. Every time. One minute late chips away at trust.

- Be emotionally present. Put down the phone. Tune out the job. Tune in to them.

Children don't remember every activity—but they remember how they felt in your presence. Were they prioritized? Or were they squeezed in?

They don't need perfection. They need to feel safe, seen, and loved. Your presence—steady and reliable—is what grounds them, especially when everything else in their world feels uncertain.

What They Learn from You

Your children are watching—even when you think they aren't. They're learning what love looks like. What strength sounds like. How partners treat each other. How a protector shows up or doesn't.

Whether you intend to or not, you're teaching them what's "normal." And psychology is clear on this: we marry what is familiar. Not necessarily what is healthy. What is familiar.

Children who grow up with emotionally distant or inconsistent parents often repeat those patterns in adulthood. Daughters, in particular, are more likely to choose partners who mirror their father's emotional availability, expressions of affection, and presence—or absence (Fraley & Shaver, 2000; Dinero et al., 2008). Attachment theory tells us that our early relationships create internal templates. If children learn to chase connection, silence their needs, or question their worth, they'll carry that into their romantic future.

But here's the good news: healthy can become familiar too. If you're present, emotionally attuned, and consistent—even after your own rough calls—they'll internalize that version of love. And that's the kind of partner they'll look for.

Families Can Heal, Too

Families can heal when they're brought into the conversation. When they're given permission to speak the hard truths. When they're not expected to just endure, but to understand.

Departments that prioritize family wellness—real family wellness—don't just reduce divorce and burnout. They build stronger officers. Better firefighters. Healthier humans. Because when your home life is stable, your performance improves. Your judgment sharpens. Your empathy returns. You become more resilient—not less—when your family isn't drowning behind you.

This is what cumulative trauma looks like when it's left untreated—when departments say "take care of yourself" but punish those who do. When therapy is optional until it's court-ordered. When peer support is more about checking a box than opening a door.

Family members begin living in a quiet kind of crisis. They adapt. They compensate. They become fluent in reading micro-expressions. They learn to avoid conflict. They over-function, under-function, or burn out. And all the while, the first responder feels more and more like a ghost in their own home.

It doesn't happen all at once. It's a slow leak. A missed dinner here. A snapped response there. A growing wall of unspoken things. Until one day, someone says the word no one wanted to say: divorce. Or rehab. Or worse.

But this is not inevitable.

Vulnerability Is a Survival Skill

The families of first responders deserve to be seen as part of the system—not as an afterthought. They need tools, education, and support, not just a department flyer and a crisis hotline. They need to know what trauma looks like in a loved one. How to stay connected without enabling. How to protect their own mental health.

And first responders need to know that being vulnerable at home is not a weakness. It's a survival skill. You can't armor up 24/7 and expect to thrive in relationships. You can't wall off your emotions and expect intimacy to grow. You can't numb selectively. If you shut down sadness, you also shut down joy.

The job may change you. But it doesn't have to cost you your family.

We heal in relationships. And that starts by naming what's really happening behind closed doors.

This chapter isn't about blame. It's about awareness. About shining a light on what gets silently carried. Because the trauma may begin on the job—but it rarely ends there.

Helping Families Stay Connected

Dr. Kevin Gilmartin, in his foundational book *Emotional Survival for Law Enforcement*, recommends taking 20 minutes after work to decompress before engaging with family. Step outside. Sit in your car. Listen to music. Shift from survival mode to human mode. But then—go inside. Be present. Your family deserves more than the leftovers of your shift (Gilmartin, 2002).

Dr. Ellen Kirschman's work, particularly in her book *I Love a Cop*, echoes this need for emotional reconnection at home and gives guidance to both officers and their partners on how to maintain intimacy and understanding in the face of occupational trauma (Kirschman, 2007).

Here are a few practical ways families can stay connected and support each other, even when the job takes a toll. These strategies don't require big changes—just small, intentional actions that build understanding and trust over time.

- **Name the weight.** You don't need to relive the call. Just saying, "It was a hard shift today," helps your family know it's not about them.

- **Use "I" statements.** "I'm overwhelmed right now." "I need 15 minutes to transition." This lowers defenses and opens connection.

- **Don't make your partner guess.** A little emotional context prevents unnecessary conflict.

- **Reconnect through small rituals.** Morning coffee, bedtime check-ins, and shared meals help rebuild connection.

- **Normalize help.** The strongest families ask for support early. Therapy, peer support, or a trusted friend—it matters.

The Birthday

It was Officer Robinson's daughter's fourteenth birthday. Balloons were up. The cake was out. The family had gathered. But he wasn't really there. He had come straight from a double shift—no time to shower, no time to shift gears. Earlier that morning, he'd responded to a suicide. A teenager. Same age as the kids at the party.

He didn't talk about it. Just said he was "tired." But the way he sat on the couch, staring through the walls, short with everyone, arms crossed, said everything.

His wife pulled him aside and asked, "What's going on?"

He paused, looked at her, and for once, didn't deflect.

"I had a rough one this morning. A kid. It's sitting heavy."

That's all he said. No details. No dramatics.

And that's all she needed. Her body softened. Her voice changed. Instead of feeling like she was fighting a ghost, she was standing next to her husband again.

No one is asking first responders to bleed their trauma out on the kitchen table. But a small window into what they're carrying can prevent a wall from forming between them and the people who love them most. Families don't need to fix it. They just need to understand it. And understanding starts with honesty — one real moment at a time.

Top 5 Takeaways for First Responder Families

First responder families face unique challenges when it comes to communication and emotional support. Open, honest conversations can make all the difference in strengthening these bonds. Here are some takeaways to help families stay connected and resilient.

1. **Say a little — even one sentence helps.** You don't need to unload the whole call. But "I had a rough shift" is better than silence.

2. **Take 20 minutes to decompress, then engage.** Gilmartin's rule works — transition from survival brain to human brain before stepping into your family space.

3. **Explain the distance.** If you're shut down, let your partner know it's emotional overload — not about them.

4. **Let the kids see the connection.** They don't need details. They need warmth, eye contact, and laughter — even if it's brief.

5. **Get support early.** Waiting until a crisis damages trust. Normalize therapy. Normalize talking. Normalize asking for help.

In the end, staying connected as a first responder family isn't about fixing every problem or always saying the perfect thing. It's about showing up for each other, being honest in small ways, and remembering that even the simplest moments of support matter. With open communication and a little understanding, families can weather the toughest days together.

Chapter 11

Healing from Administrative Betrayal

There's a unique kind of devastation that comes from being betrayed not by criminals or the public, but by your own house — by the very people who were supposed to have your back.

We sign up knowing we'll face danger on the street. That's the job. But we don't expect to be gutted from the inside out — by silence, inconsistency, unchecked ego, or apathy from above. This is **administrative betrayal**, and for many, it's the trauma that finally breaks them.

"Why Can't You Let It Go?"

One of the hardest parts of healing from bureaucratic stress is that it rarely gets acknowledged. It doesn't bleed. It doesn't come with a dramatic headline. So when officers try to talk about it, they're met with eye rolls, deflection, or "Just move on."

But here's the truth: People struggling with bureaucratic betrayal often sound obsessive — because they've been stuck in a system that **refuses to validate their reality**. They replay the story, not because they want to, but because they *have to*. It hasn't landed anywhere safe.

Family and friends get fatigued. "You've told this story already." Peers start pulling away. "That's just how the job is." And the officer is left feeling crazy, isolated, and silenced.

But they're not crazy. They're hurt. And they're not asking for pity — they're asking to be heard.

Betrayal Reopens Old Wounds

A large percentage of officers come into this profession with high ACE (Adverse Childhood Experience) scores—many carrying old traumas from chaotic, invalidating, or abusive homes. The "police family" offers something that feels stable, loyal, and honorable.

So when betrayal happens within that structure—when that "family" abandons, shames, or ignores them—it doesn't just sting in the moment. It reactivates everything from the past:

- The childhood abandonment.
- The feeling of being unseen or disposable.
- The belief that you have to be perfect to be worthy of care.

That's why it hits so hard. It's not just about the incident. It's about the **emotional core rupture** that comes with it.

What the Science Says: Moral Injury & Institutional Betrayal

Psychological research gives language to what cops have been feeling for years: this isn't just "drama" or "bitterness." It's a legitimate form of trauma.

Moral injury is the pain that comes from violating your own sense of right and wrong—or being forced to witness it. It is often accompanied by guilt, shame, or rage (Litz et al., 2009). Institutional betrayal occurs when a trusted system, like your department, fails to protect you—or even becomes a source of harm (Smith & Freyd, 2014). These two concepts help explain why the sense of betrayal in law enforcement feels so deep; it is not just an individual struggle, but also a response to being let down by the very institution meant to support you.

According to a 2023 Police1 survey of over 4,000 officers, **internal administrative stressors—not the street—were the #1 reason cops leave the profession**. This isn't a fringe issue. It's a crisis.

Therapists and clinicians also need to understand that officers wrestling with bureaucratic stress might not present like classic PTSD. They're not always tearful or shut down. More often, they're angry, ruminating, mistrusting, or emotionally flooded. They've burned out their support systems. Everyone's tired of hearing the story. But the story hasn't landed in a place where it feels seen.

That's why healing often starts not with a treatment plan, but with validation. "What happened to you was wrong." That sentence alone can be life-changing.

Strategies for Healing

Let's review some practical strategies for healing the deep wounds of moral injury and institutional betrayal. These strategies offer a path forward, transforming pain into growth and restoring a sense of hope and agency.

1. Therapy That Actually Gets It

This kind of betrayal can't be fixed by basic stress management tips or a few "deep breathing" exercises. You need a therapist who understands the culture—and the complexity.

Not every kind of therapy works for this kind of injury. Here's what actually helps:

- **EMDR (Eye Movement Desensitization and Reprocessing)** can help you reprocess the betrayal and emotional injury so it doesn't feel so raw and intrusive. It's not about forgetting—it's about loosening the grip that memory has on you.

- **DBT (Dialectical Behavior Therapy)** is useful for managing the emotional extremes that come with betrayal—especially anger, hopelessness, or the urge to shut down completely. It teaches concrete tools to stay grounded when emotions are intense.
- **ACT (Acceptance and Commitment Therapy)** helps rebuild purpose when you feel lost or disillusioned. It's not about ignoring the pain. It's about learning how to carry it while still living a life aligned with your values.
- And sometimes what you really need is a **humanistic, person-centered approach**—someone who listens, gets the culture, and doesn't try to "fix" you in the first ten minutes. Someone who can sit with your pain without trying to make it go away too fast.

2. Peer Support That Knows Its Role

The right peer supporter can be a game changer—especially one who knows how to sit with pain, not silence it. Real support means listening without judgment, validating what's real, and helping a brother or sister take the next right step—not enabling, not avoiding, but being present.

3. Leadership That Doesn't Disappear

When leaders stay engaged during the hard moments, it makes a difference. It doesn't have to be dramatic—instead, it can take the form of a brief check-in, a quiet acknowledgment, or simply making space for the conversation. A gentle invitation to a conversation, like *"I know things have been rough. Let me know how I can support you,"* can go a long way. That's not being soft. That's leadership that earns trust.

4. Education That Makes You Stronger

Officers deserve to understand how trauma actually works—including betrayal trauma, moral injury, and the damage of unchecked authority.

Not so they become therapists, but so they stop blaming themselves. So they stop thinking they're "crazy" when what they're really feeling is deeply human.

Administrative betrayal doesn't just damage morale—it damages people. It makes good cops walk away and leaves the rest wondering if the job is worth it.

But there is a path forward. It begins with validation. With truth-telling. With leadership that listens. And with officers who refuse to stay silent—not out of revenge, but out of hope that no one else has to carry the same wound alone.

Chapter 12

Building a Culture That Doesn't Eat Its Own

A Message from Lt. Chad Farley, Law Enforcement Executive:

Across this country, chiefs and command staff have done the hard, often unseen work of shifting law enforcement culture for the better. Many of you reading this have led the way in making officer wellness a real priority — by embedding clinicians, launching peer support programs, investing in leadership development, and being willing to talk openly about things that once lived only in silence. That work matters. It is saving careers — and saving lives.

This book honors that work. And it builds upon it.

Dr. Gina Gallivan's Betrayed from within *is not a critique — it's a continuation. It offers something rare and powerful: a clear, research-backed, emotionally grounded look at what still remains under the surface, even in departments that have made great progress. It gives voice to a quiet form of strain many officers carry — not just from the street, but from within the organization itself.*

If we're honest, we know it's there. It shows up in the form of disengagement, frustration, silence, or slow burnout. Often, it's not about one incident — it's about a hundred small ones. Feeling passed over. Not being heard. Seeing inconsistency in how discipline is handled. Sensing that courage and vulnerability aren't always met with support. These are all issues tied to one foundational principle: procedural justice.

Procedural justice isn't just a tool for community engagement — it's a framework for internal leadership. Officers want the same thing the public does: to be treated fairly, to have a voice, to understand how decisions are made, and to be treated with dignity, even when the answer is "no." When we deliver that, trust grows. So does performance. So does resilience.

The good news? Many of us are already moving in this direction. What this book offers is a way to take that work to the next level.

It invites us to ask powerful, courageous questions:

- *Do our promotional processes reflect transparency and equity?*
- *Do our officers know they can speak up — and be heard?*
- *Are we consistent in how we hold people accountable, no matter their popularity or position?*
- *Do our sergeants and lieutenants feel empowered to lead with empathy, not just authority?*

These aren't critiques. They're invitations. Because when leaders are willing to look inward — to apply procedural justice not just externally but internally — that's when culture truly shifts.

Dr. Gallivan's stories are raw, yes. But they are also redemptive. They show how leadership, when intentional and human, can heal even the deepest fractures in morale. They show that the culture we create is not fixed, but forged. Every decision, policy, and conversation either builds trust or compromises it.

The fact that you're reading this book is proof that you care about doing it right.

So let it affirm what you're already doing well. Let it challenge you, not in criticism, but in confidence — that you have the influence, the courage, and the vision to lead a department where procedural justice is lived out at every level, from the newest recruit to the chief's office.

Let this be a reminder: the best leaders are the ones who never stop growing.

The ones who know that culture isn't built by force – but by fairness.

That trust isn't demanded – it's earned.

And that wellness doesn't happen because of a policy – it happens because of people.

To Chiefs and Command Staff

You've read a lot so far about what goes wrong. About betrayal, burnout, bureaucracy, and the damage inflicted—sometimes unintentionally—by the very institutions meant to support first responders. But this chapter is different. This chapter is for you.

Not to point fingers—but to invite reflection. Not to accuse—but to offer insight. Not to criticize—but to help you lead better.

It's lonely at the top. Chiefs and command staff absorb pressure from both directions—officers below and politics above. You're expected to maintain morale, protect your people, balance community expectations, manage lawsuits, navigate city hall, and lead with vision—all while staying calm and composed under a microscope.

Every decision is second-guessed. Every statement is analyzed. And every misstep becomes a headline. Many chiefs lie awake at night not because they don't care—but because they do. They carry the weight of officer suicides, internal investigations, budget cuts, broken trust, and the impossible task of pleasing everyone while protecting their team.

You came up through the ranks. You remember the street. And now, you're expected to be a politician in uniform. Sometimes, that burden changes you.

The Forgotten Toll of 2020 and Beyond

After the pandemic and the wave of anti-police sentiment following George Floyd, the profession was rocked. Officers left in droves—retired early, walked away, or burned out beyond return. And the ones who stayed were told to pick up the slack.

Staffing plummeted. Morale collapsed. But the calls kept coming. And the expectation was clear: "Do more with less. And don't complain."

Some officers worked 16-hour shifts for days in a row. Canceled vacations, missed family events, ran on fumes. They weren't just tired—they were depleted. And no amount of coffee, gallows humor, or "thank you for your service" banners could refill the tank.

They were exhausted. But there was no room for that exhaustion to be named or treated—not for the officers on the street, and not for the chiefs trying to hold it all together. Just pressure to keep showing up.

Behind the scenes, chiefs and command staff were facing their own perfect storm:

- Workforce numbers dropped due to illness and psychological stress.
- Forced overtime became the norm.
- Retirements surged, and vacancies ballooned.
- Budget cuts and defunding debates left departments scrambling.
- Chiefs faced growing pressure from their own families to step down—and lost longtime friends over politics.

- Injured-on-duty claims skyrocketed.
- Referrals for alcohol misuse and inpatient psychiatric care reached record highs.

And through it all, they were expected to lead.

The toll wasn't just operational—it was deeply personal. Chiefs had to make decisions with no precedent, lead in hostile political climates, and balance their officers' well-being with the department's survival. Many suffered in silence.

Understanding this context helps reframe the internal division we often see: the rank and file feeling abandoned, and the command staff feeling overwhelmed. Both can be true.

Culture Starts with the Chief

If the rank and file are suffering in silence, look up. Culture is modeled from the top down.

- If vulnerability is mocked in the command staff, it will be buried at every level below.
- If wellness is something optional, it will be seen as a weakness.
- If retaliation is tolerated, silence will reign.

But the opposite is also true:

- If you own your mistakes, your people will too.
- If you show up to debriefs, funerals, and promotions, your people will feel seen.
- If you talk about wellness as strategy—not weakness—your people will buy in.

Discipline is part of the job. But how it's delivered matters. Officers can accept correction when it's done with fairness, clarity, and context. What breaks them is when discipline feels personal, inconsistent, or politically motivated.

If you're only visible when someone's in trouble, you're not leading—you're policing your own.

You Set the Tone for Generations

Culture isn't built in a policy manual. It's built in briefing rooms, promotional interviews, hallway conversations, and the way you talk about the last officer who took a leave of absence for mental health reasons.

Ask yourself:

- Do your people feel safe bringing bad news to you?
- Do they know how to access support without shame?
- Do your sergeants feel empowered to lead—or just afraid to screw up?

If you find gaps in your answers, don't ignore them—start small, meaningful conversations with your team. Invite honest feedback, listen without judgment, and take practical steps to address concerns. Building trust and support is ongoing work, but each action you take—no matter how minor—can make your workplace safer, healthier, and more resilient for everyone.

The best leaders are culture disruptors. They:

- Advocate for peer support—and participate in it.
- Bring therapists into the building, not just the benefits brochure.

- Take the mental temperature of their teams — not just the stats.

- Publicly support those who seek help.

- Build pathways for early intervention — not just discipline.

They know the job is hard — but they don't make it harder. Instead, they break cycles of silence by fostering openness and accountability at every level. When leaders model vulnerability and proactive support, they lay the groundwork for lasting trust, a foundation every team needs to thrive.

A Message of Hope

Leadership is hard enough — don't do it in isolation. Chiefs need to take care of each other, too. Pick up the phone. Check in. Share resources. Compare notes. If another chief is struggling, reach out before burnout, illness, or retirement forces their hand. We lose good leaders when we let them suffer alone.

If you've made mistakes, you're in good company. Every great chief I know has. But what separates the good from the great is this: they own it, learn from it, and change course.

You can lead in a way that honors your people, without compromising your role. You can call out dysfunction without burning down the system. You can build a culture that doesn't eat its own.

Start now. And they'll follow.

Chief's Checklist: Action Items for Culture Change

Let's be real—chiefs carry their own kind of burden. They're expected to be politically savvy, emotionally bulletproof, media-ready, and somehow everywhere at once. The job isn't what it used to be. Since 2020, they've faced a staffing crisis, skyrocketing public scrutiny, political interference, and internal fractures—all while trying to hold the line.

Some chiefs inherit broken cultures. Some are trying to lead from the middle—squeezed between city managers, unions, and a generation of officers barely holding on. Many want to do the right thing but are one misstep away from losing the trust of their people *or* their job.

That doesn't excuse poor leadership. But it does explain why some leaders shut down, retreat, or protect the wrong people.

This checklist isn't about blame. It's a blueprint for the chiefs who care but are exhausted, isolated, or unsure where to start. For the ones who show up to peer support trainings, who walk into briefings when morale is low, who know that culture isn't fixed by a memo—it's built, day by day, through presence and integrity.

1. **Be Visible and Approachable**
   Walk through roll calls. Attend debriefs. Know your people by name.

2. **Normalize Mental Health Support**
   Share your own story. Talk openly about therapy, wellness, and resilience.

3. **Audit Your Disciplinary Process**
   Look for patterns of inconsistency, retaliation, or excessive punishment.

4. **Invest in Peer Support**
   Train, fund, and empower peer teams. Don't let them become performative—they should be active, respected, and fully integrated into the wellness fabric of the agency.

5. **Promote Based on Integrity, Not Popularity**
   Leadership should reflect competence and character—not politics.

6. **Protect Whistleblowers**
   Have a zero-tolerance policy for retaliation. Speak up when someone's integrity is punished.

7. **Hold Power-Trippers Accountable**
   Don't allow unchecked egos or toxic personalities to corrode morale. Call out bullying and abuse of power early—before it spreads.

8. **Encourage Exit Interviews**
   Learn why good people leave—and fix what you can.

9. **Recognize the Emotional Labor of the Job**
   Support spouses, children, and families. Create programming that includes them.

10. **Model the Behavior You Expect**
    Your tone becomes the culture. Your silence becomes permission.

11. **Honor Peer Support Teams Publicly**
    Follow the example of leaders like Chief Ed Medrano, who made it a point to attend the beginning of every quarterly Peer Support

training at Gardena PD. He didn't just show up—he spoke to the team, affirmed their value, and reminded them how essential they are to the department's health. That kind of visible support builds legitimacy and morale.

12. **Show Up When It Counts**
    After a shooting or officer-involved incident, call the officer. If someone's injured, show up at the hospital. When your staff tells you that a captain is milking it to retirement while others suffer, take it seriously. Ignoring it erodes trust.

13. **Stay Humble**
    Culture is a living thing. Keep learning. Keep listening. Keep leading.

As leaders and peers, your daily choices shape the heart of your agency. Remember: lasting change isn't just about policy—it's about people. Lead with compassion, hold one another up, and never underestimate the power of showing up when it matters most.

Conclusion

You Can Heal Without Their Apology

You did everything right. You showed up. You backed your partners. You gave the job everything you had—sometimes at the expense of your health, your family, and your sense of self. And somewhere along the way, the job stopped giving back.

This book wasn't written to diagnose you. It was written to name what no one else would:

That sometimes, it's not the street that breaks you. It's your own leadership. That betrayal from within the ranks cuts deeper than anything the public could throw at you. And when that betrayal hits—it doesn't just bruise your ego.

It reopens old wounds.

What Gets Triggered

Sometimes, when you're gaslit by people you once respected or punished for speaking the truth, when you give your all and receive only silence in return, the pain doesn't just stay within the department—it lingers, echoing into other corners of your life. These moments awaken deeper wounds: the father who never showed up, the teacher who humiliated you in front of the class, the bullies who taught you early on that speaking up only made things worse, and the parent whose love felt like a prize you had to earn.

That's the hidden weight so many carry. The system is often blind to the fact that it's poking at wounds that were barely stitched closed, intensifying hurts that reach far beyond today's uniform or badge.

But here's the truth: you are not just a product of what happened to you. You're responsible for what you do next. Because if you're not careful, the betrayal becomes your identity. You start to expect disappointment. You stop trusting anyone. You pull back from people who care because you don't want to be let down again.

That's not protection. That's learned helplessness. And it doesn't just rob you of healing—it makes you someone others start to tiptoe around. You may have been victimized. But you don't have to live like a victim.

Your Greatest Weapon

The tactical brain understands this: what you think determines how you fight. Just like you train your body, you can train your thoughts. And that starts with this truth: *Pain is information. It's not your whole identity.* Use it.

Mental toughness isn't about shutting down emotion—it's about directing it with purpose.

As Navy SEAL David Goggins said:

"You are in danger of living a life so comfortable and soft, that you will die without ever realizing your true potential" (Goggins, 2018, *Can't Hurt Me*).

You didn't go through all of this to stay bitter. You went through it to gain clarity. To grow stronger. To be the kind of leader or partner you wish you had.

Spiritual Growth Through Adversity

Pain breaks some people. It builds others. And for some, it opens a door. What you do with that pain is up to you. You can let it hold you back, or you can let it shape you into someone wiser and more resilient.

Spiritual growth isn't about religion. It's about meaning. Somewhere in this mess, you may have found out who you *really* are. You may have learned how not to treat people. You may now understand the damage of indifference and the power of kindness that shows up unannounced.

Maybe, just maybe, none of this happened *to* you. Maybe it happened *for* you. So that when you get the chance to lead, you lead differently.

When You Promote — You'll Know

When the time finally comes for you to be promoted, I hope that you'll remember what it felt like to be ignored. To be skipped over. To sit in silence while others laughed behind closed doors. To be strong enough to keep showing up, even when no one said thank you.

And I hope that memory will become your guide. You'll spot those officers who are barely holding on. You'll hear the silence between their words. And you'll *see* them. That's what good leadership does. It breaks the cycle.

It's easy to let the pain of the past harden your heart, to put up walls and convince yourself that caring is a weakness. But the truth is, the experiences that hurt us most can also be the ones that open us up to real empathy. When you reach out a hand to someone who's struggling, you're not only helping them — you're reminding yourself that the world can be better, that dignity and kindness still matter in a place that sometimes forgets both.

Maybe you never received a word of encouragement when you needed it most. Now, you have the chance to become the leader who offers it freely. Every small act of understanding — a genuine question, a listening ear, a simple "I've been there" — can be a turning point in someone's life. Your scars give you insight, and your willingness to care can create the kind of workplace you once wished for. In leading with compassion, you mend not just your own story, but the story of those who come after you.

Bottom Line

You don't need their apology to heal. You don't need the system to change to start showing up differently. You don't need permission to begin again.

You just need to choose: Not to let bitterness win. Not to let betrayal write the rest of your story.

Not to let what *they* did become who *you* are.

Healing doesn't erase the past—it transforms it.

And what comes next? That's yours to write.

My Letter to the Officer Who Stayed Too Long in a Broken System

You gave everything. Your loyalty. Your sleep. Your time with family. You played by the rules. Backed your partners. Took the overtime. Ate the disrespect. Smiled when you should've spoken up. Stayed when you should've walked.

And somehow, you're the one who got hurt.

Maybe they retaliated when you spoke the truth. Maybe they promoted someone less qualified but better connected. Maybe they told you to be ethical, then punished you for doing exactly that.

Now you walk in bitter, numb, or pissed off—wondering when it all changed.

If that's you, read this carefully:

You're not crazy. You're not weak. You're not alone.

What happened to you wasn't just frustrating. It was a betrayal. A betrayal of the ideals you swore to uphold. A betrayal by the people who were supposed to lead with integrity.

You are not imagining it.

And you don't need to "get over it."

But you do need to move through it.

Because if you stay stuck in resentment, they still own you. If you check out completely, they win.

So here's what I want you to hear:

You're right. That wasn't okay. You got wronged. You were loyal to people who weren't loyal to you. That should never have happened. And you have every right to be angry.

You are not your badge. You're more than this department. More than your last eval. More than the politics that sidelined you. You're a father. A sister. A fighter. A human being. The badge should've been an extension of who you are – not the definition.

Use the pain to lead differently. If you stay, lead better. If you promote, promote with honor. If you mentor someone, do it with truth. Let this betrayal refine your character, not rot your outlook. Be the leader you never had.

Get your anger out. Then get clear. Yell. Vent. Write it out. But don't stay there. Decide what you stand for now. Protect your peace. Be intentional about how you show up. You owe that to yourself and your people.

Control what you can. Release what you can't. You can't fix a broken command staff. You can't force someone to act with integrity. But you can protect your mindset. Your health. Your home life. That's where your real power is.

You're still needed. Don't let them convince you otherwise. You still matter. You still make a difference. You still have value. Even if you never get the promotion. Even if they never say thank you.

Healing doesn't mean forgetting. It means carrying the lesson, not the wound.

And if no one else ever says it –

Thank you for staying as long as you did. Now it's time to heal.

Not because they deserve your forgiveness. But because you deserve your freedom.

Dr. Gina Gallivan is a Licensed *(CA PSY#PSY18184)* and Board-Certified (ABPP, 2012) Police and Public Safety Psychologist with over 20 years of experience supporting the mental health and wellness of first responders. She has served as an Executive Board Member and General Chair of the Psychological Services Section of the International Association of Chiefs of Police (IACP). Currently, she chairs the IACP Police Officer Wellness Initiative Committee and actively contributes to several others, including the Peer Support and Fitness for Duty Guidelines Committees, as well as the Officer Safety and Wellness Suicide Prevention Committee.

Dr. Gallivan's expertise in public safety mental health has made her a sought-after trainer at the city, state, national, and international levels. She is the founder of Southern California's Regional Peer Support Program and provides peer support training and program management for public safety agencies across the region.

Dr. Gallivan's foundation in Police Psychology began with her training at the Los Angeles County Sheriff's Department. Since then, she has provided psychological services to over 100 police and public safety agencies in Southern California. As a California Peace Officers Standards and Training (P.O.S.T.)

subject matter expert and an approved evaluator, she has conducted more than 15,000 pre-employment psychological screenings for first responders.

Beyond her contributions to preventative care, Dr. Gallivan has been a primary trauma responder for numerous critical incidents. These include some of the most significant events in recent history, such as the Seal Beach Salon Meritage mass shooting, the Santa Monica active shooter incident, the UCLA active shooter, the Christopher Dorner active shooter and manhunt, the Route 91 Las Vegas concert mass shooting, the Thousand Oaks Borderline Bar and Grill mass shooting, and the Huntington Beach Police Department helicopter crash line-of-duty death.

Dr. Gallivan's extensive experience, leadership in public safety psychology, and unwavering commitment to the wellness of first responders make her a trusted voice and authority in trauma recovery and resilience. As a cancer survivor and mother of three children, Dr. Gallivan brings a deeply personal understanding of resilience, healing, and the demands of balancing family and professional life.

www.firstresponderpsych.com

Acknowledgments

I want to acknowledge my mother-in-law, **Nancy Gallivan,** whose leadership, emotional intelligence, and ability to hold a large family together have been nothing short of extraordinary. As the mother of seven and grandmother of twenty-six, she has cultivated a family rooted in faith, strong values, and deep connection. There is no divorce, no fractured relationships, no drama—just unity, respect, and mutual support. And she is the one who steers that ship with strength and purpose.

While writing about the damage caused by poor leadership and toxic systems, I often found myself reflecting on her example—the opposite of dysfunction. A true matriarch who leads without ego, resolves conflict without drama, and role-models maturity, integrity, and decisive leadership. She shows what it means to lead with conviction and consistency. It has been a privilege to witness the lasting impact of a life lived with such strength and clarity.

I extend my deepest gratitude to my mentors, Dr. Jocelyn Roland, Dr. Larry Blum, Dr. Kathleen Pollock, and Dr. Phil Trompetter, whose guidance and wisdom paved the way for my career. Your dedication to the field of public safety psychology has been instrumental in shaping my path, and I am forever grateful for your influence.

A special thank you to Drs. Lewis Schlosser and Brian Mangan for their professional development support, and to retired Hawthorne Police Sergeant Gabe Lira and Lt. Chad Farley.

Lt. Chad Farley helped spark the regional peer support concept when he contacted me following the Route 91 mass shooting, requesting I facilitate a debriefing for affected law enforcement personnel. That day, I led a powerful conversation—and among the officers present were several peer support team members I had trained from surrounding agencies. I watched them step up, share their stories, and hold space for one another. It was a profound moment that revealed the healing power of interagency, peer-driven support.

I wanted to make this form of mutual emotional aid sustainable. So I brought together the leaders of each agency's peer support team—agencies I had trained and was overseeing at the time. One of our team members suggested creating a WhatsApp group to streamline communication, something we had done within agencies before. This time, it crossed department lines. It wasn't an intra-agency model like what had been done at a larger sheriff's department. What made this different—and special—was that it was **inter-agency**.

The first formal regional response happened after a line-of-duty death at the Gardena Police Department. That's where the vision became reality. I will never forget watching Gabe Lira grab a notepad, calmly begin organizing peer support shifts, asking what food, water, or presence needed to be delivered. No ego. Just clarity, leadership, and love in action.

Shortly after that initial response at Gardena PD, there was a suicide at the Long Beach Police Department. A colleague of mine was servicing that department during the call. I reached out to her directly and shared the idea behind our regional peer support deployment—how well it had worked during the Gardena response, and how we had organized teams from surrounding agencies to provide emotional aid. I offered to send my teams to support Long Beach. She agreed, and we responded.

That deployment helped the idea grow even further. What began as a small act of interagency collaboration became a sustainable model—because we were filling a real need. Departments needed help, and we had created a way to give it without red tape and without delay.

This is how the Southern California regional peer support model truly began—not through a task force or official committee, but through action. What made this different—and special—was that it involved outside agencies stepping up for one another. That mutual aid component was entirely new at the time. It created safety nets for departments that didn't have internal support and built bridges between agencies that had never coordinated peer support in this way before.

Gabe took the seed of an idea and brought it to life. He led the coordination of our Southern California regional peer support model—responding to middle-of-the-night calls, managing highly emotional scenes, and building a network of mutual aid that has since been replicated across the country.

His leadership didn't just operationalize a system—it built trust. It fostered belonging. It created a legacy of care for wounded first responders.

Thank you, Gabe. Your strength and humility helped turn vision into reality—and in doing so, brought healing to countless lives.

"Matty" Fiorenza, featured in the film PTSD911, continues to change lives through his advocacy, his vulnerability, and his tireless work in creating wellness-forward cultures within first responder agencies. His willingness to lead with authenticity has brought hope and direction to many.

Each of these individuals has contributed something essential to the movement of first responder wellness—and I am deeply grateful for their impact, heart, and leadership.

Additionally, I want to recognize and express my deepest gratitude to the dedicated peer support leaders in Southern California who have gone above and beyond, quite literally saving the lives of their fellow first responders. Among them, Jim Uhl, Sam Reed, Mark Wersching, Raul Alarcon, Stuart Scott, Chad Farley, Brian Seitz, Matt Fiorenza, Gabe Lira, Angela Balzano, Ish Ververa, and Kelly Benjamin have been instrumental in life-saving efforts. Their unwavering commitment, compassion, and tireless advocacy have made an immeasurable impact on countless lives. While there are too many to name who have provided significant assistance, these individuals stand out for their extraordinary dedication to their brothers and sisters in public safety. For your continued professional support and collaboration—your insights, expertise, and encouragement mean more than words can express.

I also want to acknowledge the many police chiefs who took risks to implement wellness programs for their employees at a time when it was not yet common practice. In particular, Police Chief Darren Arakawa, for the numerous times he presented with me at IACP. His presentation inspired chiefs from around the country to implement wellness programs, leaving a lasting impact on law enforcement wellness nationwide. Eugene "Top" Harris, who generously volunteered his time on numerous occasions to teach the stress management techniques from his book, *The Zero Stress Zone*. Your commitment to officer well-being has made a lasting impact.

I am also deeply grateful to the team of culturally competent clinicians at my practice. They are among the best in the field, and I am lucky to work with them. Their tireless dedication, clinical excellence, and heart-centered service save lives and elevate the standard of care for the first responder community every single day.

I would be remiss not to thank Karla Macareno, my assistant, office manager, and the true boss of the company. Karla works tirelessly to ensure our first responder agencies are supported with care and precision. Her dedication, positive spirit, and grace under pressure keep everything running smoothly. She brings warmth and joy to everyone she meets and has become like family to me. Karla, thank you for being the heart of this mission.

I offer my heartfelt gratitude to Father Paul Sustayta, pastor of Blessed Sacrament Catholic Church, whose presence and wisdom have been a light during times of deep reflection and healing. Your faith, compassion, and unwavering commitment to service have reminded me that true leadership is found in humility, and that healing often begins in silence, stillness, and sacred connection. Thank you for holding space for those who carry invisible wounds. Your words and your walk continue to inspire me — and so many others — to lead with grace and love.

I also want to thank Lia Ottaviano, my developmental editor, whose thoughtful feedback, editorial skill, and dedication to this project were instrumental in bringing clarity and cohesion to these pages. Her contribution helped ensure that the message of this book resonates with the very people it was written for.

To my family, especially my parents, my brother, my sister, aunts, uncles, in-laws, cousins, and my beloved nieces and nephews — family is everything to me. Thank you for instilling in me strong morals, ethics, faith, and a steadfast work ethic. Your unwavering love and support laid the foundation for everything I have achieved. Mom — I know you have a front-row seat to what I am doing. I hope I am making you proud.

Finally, to my best friend and husband, Michael Gallivan, and my wonderful children, Michael Jr., Sophia, and Julia — you are the center of my universe, my inspiration, and my heart. I thank God for you every day. Your love and support fuel my passion and purpose, and I am eternally grateful for the gift of our family.

References

Chapter 2

Litz, B. T., Stein, N., Delaney, E., Lebowitz, L., Nash, W. P., Silva, C., & Maguen, S. (2009). Moral injury and moral repair in war veterans: A preliminary model and intervention strategy. *Clinical Psychology Review*, 29(8), 695–706. https://doi.org/10.1016/j.cpr.2009.07.003

Williamson, V., Murphy, D., & Greenberg, N. (2020). COVID-19 and experiences of moral injury in front-line key workers. *Occupational Medicine*, 70(5), 317–319. https://doi.org/10.1093/occmed/kqaa052

Chapter 4

Rosenthal, S. A., & Pittinsky, T. L. (2006). Narcissistic leadership. *The Leadership Quarterly*, 17(6), 617–633. https://doi.org/10.1016/j.leaqua.2006.10.005

Chapter 5

Figley, C. R. (1995). *Compassion fatigue: Coping with secondary traumatic stress disorder in those who treat the traumatized.* Brunner-Routledge.

Follette, V. M., Polusny, M. M., & Milbeck, K. (1994). Mental health and law enforcement professionals: Trauma history, psychological symptoms, and impact of providing services to child sexual abuse survivors. *Professional Psychology: Research and Practice*, 25(3), 275–282.

Violanti, J. M., Owens, S. L., Fekedulegn, D., Ma, C. C., & Charles, L. E. (2018). Law enforcement suicide: A review. *Policing: An International Journal*, 41(5), 672–688.

Chapter 6

Litz, B. T., Stein, N., Delaney, E., Lebowitz, L., Nash, W. P., Silva, C., & Maguen, S. (2009). Moral injury and moral repair in war veterans: A preliminary model and intervention strategy. *Clinical Psychology Review*, 29(8), 695–706. https://doi.org/10.1016/j.cpr.2009.07.003

Papazoglou, K., & Andersen, J. P. (2014). A guide to utilizing police training as a tool to promote resilience and improve health outcomes among police officers. *Traumatology*, 20(2), 103–111. https://doi.org/10.1037/h0099394

Chapter 7

Edmondson, A. (1999). Psychological safety and learning behavior in work teams. *Administrative Science Quarterly*, 44(2), 350–383.

Herman, J. L. (1992). T*rauma and recovery: The aftermath of violence – from domestic abuse to political terror*. Basic Books.

Kouzes, J. M., & Posner, B. Z. (2017). T*he leadership challenge: How to make extraordinary things happen in organizations* (6th ed.). Jossey-Bass.

McAdams, D. P. (2001). The psychology of life stories. *Review of General Psychology*, 5(2), 100–122.

Chapter 8

Litz, B. T., Stein, N., Delaney, E., Lebowitz, L., Nash, W. P., Silva, C., & Maguen, S. (2009). Moral injury and moral repair in war veterans: A preliminary model and intervention strategy. *Clinical Psychology Review*, 29(8), 695–706.

Papazoglou, K., & Andersen, J. P. (2014). A guide to utilizing police training as a tool to promote resilience and improve health outcomes among police officers. *Traumatology*, 20(2), 103–111.

Shane, J. M. (2010). Organizational stressors and police performance. *Journal of Criminal Justice*, 38(4), 807–818.

Violanti, J. M. (2020). Dying for the Job: Psychological Stress and Suicide in Law Enforcement. *Charles C Thomas Publisher*.

Violanti, J. M., Owens, S. L., McCanlies, E., & Fekedulegn, D. (2017). Law enforcement work and alcohol use: A study of US police officers. *The American Journal of Industrial Medicine*, 60(5), 448–455.

Chapter 9

Dinero, R. E., Conger, R. D., Shaver, P. R., Widaman, K. F., & Larsen-Rife, D. (2008). Influence of family of origin and adult romantic partners on romantic attachment security. *Journal of Family Psychology*, 22(4), 622–632.

Fraley, R. C., & Shaver, P. R. (2000). Adult romantic attachment: Theoretical developments, emerging controversies, and unanswered questions. *Review of General Psychology*, 4(2), 132–154.

Gilmartin, K. M. (2002). *Emotional Survival for Law Enforcement: A Guide for Officers and Their Families*. E-S Press.

Kirschman, E. (2007). *I Love a Cop: What Police Families Need to Know* (2nd ed.). Guilford Press.

Spinazzola, J., Hodgdon, H., Liang, L.-J., Ford, J. D., Layne, C. M., Pynoos, R., ... & van der Kolk, B. A. (2014). Unseen wounds: The contribution of psychological maltreatment to child and adolescent mental health and risk outcomes. *Psychological Trauma: Theory, Research, Practice, and Policy,* 6(S1), S18–S28.

Teicher, M. H., & Samson, J. A. (2016). Annual research review: Enduring neurobiological effects of childhood abuse and neglect. *Journal of Child Psychology and Psychiatry,* 57(3), 241–266.

Chapter 10

Keltner, D. (2016). *The Power Paradox: How We Gain and Lose Influence.* Penguin Press.

Rosenthal, S. A., & Pittinsky, T. L. (2006). Narcissistic leadership. *The Leadership Quarterly,* 17(6), 617–633. https://doi.org/10.1016/j.leaqua.2006.10.005

Conclusion

Goggins, D. (2018). *Can't hurt me: Master your mind and defy the odds.* Lioncrest Publishing.

Recommended Reading: You're Not Alone

If you've felt the quiet, corrosive weight of internal stress—if you've questioned your sanity, your loyalty, or your place in this profession—you're not alone. These books offer insight, validation, and support for those carrying the unseen injuries of service. Some focus on culture, others on healing. All aim to help you survive the job without losing yourself.

On Leadership, Culture, and Organizational Stress

- *Emotional Survival for Law Enforcement* – *Kevin M. Gilmartin, Ph.D.*

  A foundational text for understanding burnout, hypervigilance, and the long emotional tail of public safety work.

- *The Courageous Police Leader* – *Travis Yates*

  Explores what ethical, effective leadership looks like—especially when the culture pushes for comfort or conformity.

- *Moral Injury And Policing* – *Clare Farmer & Jennifer Brown*

  A deeper look at how moral conflict and organizational betrayal affect officers' mental health and identity.

- *Breaking Ranks* – *Norm Stamper*

  A former police chief discusses systemic and internal dysfunction within departments, along with paths for reform.

On Trauma, Recovery, and Alcohol in Public Safety

- **Unbreakable: A First Responder's Guide to Healing Trauma and Finding Strength**

A culturally grounded, evidence-based roadmap for surviving trauma and reclaiming wellness. Written specifically for first responders, it offers real tools for recovery without the clinical fluff.

- *Between the Calls: Alcohol, Trauma, and Recovery in the First Responder World*

  Examines the deeply ingrained drinking culture in public safety, the trauma-alcohol loop, and how to break free without losing your identity or career. Written with honesty, empathy, and firsthand understanding.

- *The Body Keeps the Score* – Bessel Van Der Kolk, M.D.

  Explains how trauma embeds in the body and brain—and how recovery is possible through EMDR, movement, mindfulness, and other somatic modalities.

- *Unbroken Brain* – Maia Szalavitz

  A powerful reframe of addiction as a learning disorder, rooted in early trauma and emotional pain—not moral failure.

- *This Naked Mind* – Annie Grace

  A science-informed, nonjudgmental guide for anyone reevaluating their relationship with alcohol. Practical, honest, and empowering.

- *Bulletproof Spirit* – Dan Willis

  A wellness guide for law enforcement that offers emotional, physical, and spiritual tools for long-term resilience.

www.ingramcontent.com/pod-product-compliance
Lightning Source LLC
Chambersburg PA
CBHW062118080426
42734CB00012B/2911